To Lecia, for reading my first poems

and to my mother, for reading to me.

I.

ARCHAEOLOGY

WAR AT HOME: SIX STUDIES

1. ~

What if the worst damage was from / the silence about the damage / What if I told you it *was* the children / What if I told you the parents knew / What if, once, the knife was at the throat / of the mother / but the mother wouldn't call it a knife, / instead kept saying Put down that banana / What if now that I have sons myself / I mishandle them / What if in the blare of my ordinary anger / they hear the red and / blue sirens from inside my own / memories, feel the house surrounded, men / in the bushes

2. ~

if I say domestic violence   maybe you think   of the guy who takes his   girlfriend
          by the ears and   smashes the back   of her head against the bricks
as a kid shakes   an etch-a-sketch when he can't produce   the image he was after
              or maybe you think of   the girl   how huge
          her mouth becomes when she's   screaming like that, without   sound, just the triplet
thunk   of her skull, the frenzied   recognition   in her hard eyes
          but who I think of   is the little   witness looking through   the doorjamb
clutching his own   ears, so slight   he could slip through   that crack and enter
                  the room to drape himself   between the girl and   his brother's rage
          and will in his mind   a hundred thousand times   all but the time
it really happened

3. ~

can you flee wretchedness
or will it stay on you like the piquant
smoke of a crawfish boil
such that everywhere you go
people know where you've been

will it stow away and nest
in your attic growing thick & mottled
until one day, say about spring
you go rooting around in there
reach barehanded into a box

why not welcome the bite
what if that's the only way
to get it out your system
let the poison do its job
you'll either die or somebody
will finally intervene

4. ~

is there enough abuse here yet / to go around / please print your violation on the lanyard / can we at last / speak plainly of what all happened / who did what and / what it meant / let's go around the living room / raise your hand if you were just a kid / raise your hand if it wasn't your fault / you were just a kid / when that happened to you / when you did it / raise your hand please / please / we need a better grammar of shame / I can't tell / who is the subject and who is the object here / and wasn't that the problem all along

5. ~

the bad thing which poses as play
         as playing
                        one does not frequently perceive oneself as being played upon
                                one perceives oneself playing with
         one plays
                   play for instance doctor
         come crawl in here let's play doctor
                   now play you're a girl
                            now I'm the girl
no, like this
         isn't this fun
                   like when we play killing
         cowboy indian cop & robber, chase me, bang bang, blow
my fucking brains out, we're just kids,
         the hands around my throat
                        are ignorant and small

6. ~

once, in the backyard, I hit my brother square
in the head with a baseball bat. it was
an accident. it made a dull sound like *thonk*
and then he took off, carving figure-eights
in the grass at terrific speed, hand to ringing
skull, like some malfunctioning cartoon robot
tossing sparks, or maybe like that bad coyote
only all alone, no clever bird smirking from

behind a rock, just me, frightened I'd hurt
him, and he'd come for me, but he did not,
he didn't know I was there anymore, he toured
his own country of pain, an ecstatic, it wasn't
so different from what became of our lives

GOSPEL OF THE SECRET SUPPER

My middle school teacher liked
to have us boys sleep over
after bible study, after all the singing
and snacks and stripping of young souls
to wrestle on his living room carpet
while he sat erect in the recliner
in his soccer shorts and bare feet
lording over us as we pounced
and mauled each other, his mustache
glistening wet

Earlier that evening I had testified,
swung my hand high and cried out
my brother, my brother… please
lord jesus take his soul, Something
vast and complicated seized me then
as the middle school teacher banged
on the piano and our raw voices shook
Kids were always crying righteous
tears at that place as if the sorrow
we liked to gin up for the people
who weren't there would protect us
from the oily night sliding in under the edges
of the teacher's house, the night where all
the people who weren't there roamed
like swine in their delirium

When the middle school teacher put his
palm up my thigh and said Let's
pray, we were cross-legged on his bed
he'd brought me back to his room alone
I'd really only come that night
to see some girls, I was weeping
because my soul was in such jeopardy
he'd told me so, I was close to the mouth
of hell I was an emergency, I bet
when he touched the flesh of my thigh
he thought how like a pool of fire

SCHERZO FOR CHILDREN

Mother buys a house
and puts us in it.
We are little, without capital
and under-gunned.
Mother's arsenal:
one scimitar
one Remington thirty-aught six
tear gas.

My brother wields the magnifying glass
prances about the burning fiasco
on our lawn like a short and hatless witch.
All summer he makes bad fires
yet sustains no bodily harm.
A genius of his.
Still, the specter of his toasted skin
seared eyelashes, simmered bone
rankles Mother. She shouts
"No more queering around."

The scandal of the hand grenades.
I catch him stashing them
inside the lawnmower bag.
When he sees me, he throws
his head back, opens his mouth
like a chimp, waves his arms
as if he must, must fly.

To keep us safe
Mother secures the house with barbed wire
on the inside.
This reduces our chance of a puppy
to zero percent.
I blame our doglessness on my brother,
his chimp face.
Time passes. No one falls in love.
The trees outside

go green, yellow, bone, then wet bone
as per my research.
We have a whole yellow closet of *National Geographic*.
My brother trains the hairdryer still on his scalp
watches closely in the mirror. He needs
to know the melting point of brain.

Malaised, I ask my mother for a fish.
She gives the knob
on tear gas canister 21b
a half-twist.
I say the fish could easily live in the bathtub.
I say this has a certain whimsy
a certain *joie de vivre*.
I say piranhas seem like suitable pets
for children of my cohort.
She buys me a piano.

We are starved.
We gnaw old pigeon parts.
Mother, an erudite woman, says
"Eat whatsoever you may kill."
I kill lobster risotto with an orange anise sauce.
I kill starfish ravioli and vampire squid tartare.
My brother goes full loon when I do not split the yield.
Fire in the hole.

Scimitar night at our house!
The object is to hold the scimitar long enough
to make everyone go quiet when you scream
"This game does not have *joie de vivre*!"
I reach for the phone but it's not a real phone.
It's a fish, slippery and sharp, thickly alive in my palm.

Mother glares at me over her goggles
mouths *ungrateful*, chambers
a round in the Remington.
It was then that certain things ensued, got strange.
It was the final scimitar night we ever got to have.

Time passes. —*National Geographic*
Just Mother and me in the house these days.
She only speaks Fish now
there's one installed in every room
she carries on an idle conversation with the deep.
I am quiet as the bottom of the sea.

Except when I practice the piano:
mazurkas, barcarolle, the polonaise!
I'm getting quite good for my cohort.

The scherzo has a certain *joie de vivre*.
If I play loud enough?
If I pound the bass clef chords like a nightstorm
wrenching the sea from itself if I play
loud enough the whole house buzzes.
The barbed wire scrapes the skin from the walls.

THE METAPHYSICIAN CALLS
HIS MOTHER FROM JAIL

Mama can't you see the night is a dragon wing,
a veined and hideous curtain between us and the un-

conditional night beyond? The one of delicate
stars. Not for us, the dominion of the good.

But what are you offering now? And how much
real will it cost? Metaphysically, I am overdrawn.

Judge Whiskers had me explicate *agape*. To wit:
you you you. And lo, I was disabused of my right

to behold the sky. So cold in here. The blanket
they assigned me is a damp spiderweb.

I'm sorry it hurts you that we cannot worship
the god of the moon together. I'm sorry the moon

isn't real. I'm sorry you have a son who is.

There is a creature in our ceiling. All morning we've listened to it stalk the dark terrain above our heads. It scrambles it chuckles it goes boom boom thunk. I boondoggle my big brother into pulling search/destroy.

*

"Coward," I say. "The creature in our ceiling frightens you." My brother eyeballs me. He's thinking of what I'd look like dressed in a flag. Now I'm thinking of that too. How he'd lay me in state on the coffee table, wait for Lieutenant Granny to come in and whistle Taps.

*

"Maybe supper first," I say. "How do victuals sound to your person?" "Where the hooch-girl get to?" he inquires, meaning our mother, though he knows full well what's become of her. I say, "She rotated back to the World." He snorts, puts his ear to the wall.

*

"The creature is nonplussed," I say. "It won't hold back much longer." He asks if the hoochgirl left us chop-chop, and doubletimes it to the kitchen. His bare feet smack the linoleum; he slams the microwave door; I patrol his room for IEDs. What's beneath his bed? A deck of cards with hairy women; a box of birdshot; Mother's watch.

*

At table he's requisitioned my bowl of pinto beans. "To where, if it's Mister Charlie or Johnny Jihad up there?" he slurps, "all comes down to *is it him* or *is it me*." I tell him I could not say it better.

*

The ceremony of arming himself. He's hidden weapons everywhere: hamper, drawer of stove, bible cabinet, a paint can on a string hanging out of the upper window.

*

"We will not have a clusterfuck on our hands," he says. "Omaha Beach," I counsel, "Khe Sanh." His deerbow is painted pearl gray, his arrowtip is dipped in arsenic. The knife in his teeth has teeth.

A bad blast from above. We scamper into Mother's LZ, dive beneath her bed. We listen to each other breathe.

My brother stands on Mother's bed, notches an arrow and flexes the bow, squints down his shaft to the bull of my nose. "Ten-hut, pussy." His eyes, panic flares. He basks in the grandeur of the moment. "I am not afraid," he says to me. "That is a Rog," I say. "Now you get on up there most ricky-tick, sir."

It is not Mister Charles in our ceiling, or the Red Menace, or a whitefaced rapist in floppy shoes. The secret we both know is that nothing so beautiful as a person will ever again engage our lines. The creature is but an animal, unbeautiful, and my brother, lance corporal of the idiot brigade has positioned the ladder and humped in through the air duct. I remain below, peering up at the dark square.

My brother looks down at me, a line of drool swinging off his blade. He takes the knife from his teeth and pokes the cotton candy foam. "Hey, rear-echelon motherfucker, run and fetch me a torch," he says. "Ten-four," I say, and slide the grate back, and carefully twist in the screws.

REVELATION BLUES

1. See See Rider

I walked the rim of the park all night, looking for the right horse. By the Plaza the hansom cabs lined up like hopefuls in the steampunk pageant. The night was not a Dickensian violet. I had many of Caesar's coins in my purse. Later, alone with the horse, I asked him to tell me about the Andalusian mesa. "Seen one mesa, seen them all," said the horse. "You seem like a horse of integrity," I said. "I'll look you up when the atrocities resume." When, from behind his ear, I brandished a silver dollar and held it up in the moonlight, he went yet deeper in his sorrow. "The world is ending," he said. "And they're all of them blaming me."

2. Dark Was the Night Cold Was the Ground

In the spring of that year I gave birth to my own father. I ascended the C train steps at W.
81st and there he stood, smothered in amniotic fluid. We greeted each other like comrades
and went inside the museum. "The dinosaurs were here for 165 million years, achieving
nothing," he said. "QED there is no God." Someone took a photo of my father and me
frowning in front of the stegosaurus. "We created God because we know we will die, and for
no other reason," I told the person who took the picture, adding "The derelict world persists
in both directions." The photographer slapped my father, who began, at once, to cry.

3. Boom Boom Out Go the Lights

I had an ugly need and an hour to kill so I headed to Eighth Avenue. Apocalypses everywhere, times were emptying out. Three hundred bucks got me fifteen minutes of dry-hump in a mirrored closet. Her Balkans accent slipped, she would not cede the ultimate G-string. "Eet is law here," she said, half successfully. Our reflection: two hundred thousand arms, a hundred thousand breasts, a dawning of the worst of everything. "I was led to believe that three slabs of honey would rent for us a lawless zone," I said. "A state of blessedness, a kind of open city." Her gyrations turned sympathetic. "Eet ees not." After a while, of course, it began to hurt. "Do whatever you want to our bodies," I said, "besides this." So I wouldn't mistake it for spite, she used something silk to bind my hands.

4. Honey Hush

For my last meal I requested Memphis women and fried chicken. "You're a murderer, fine," they said, "but must you use these sensual words?" My abominable demands had only begun. "I crave the hot flesh of Corpus Christi and the smell of suntan oil, bring me slices of salted cucumber and hummus, strap me down and get me pegged by a Porteña tango teacher who giggles uncontrollably, give me melted butter on rye." I shook the bars of Zion's gate. "Blackberries and rosehip tea. The prophetic journals of a girl named Càterine. Kill me good as you're capable. (Let me be eight years old, climbing the loftiest branch of the apple tree with a barefoot green-eyed girl.) Fry my brains and have the elder angels weep. Bring me two cigarettes O Lord and a tumbler of scotch. I am a sick and splendid animal, king of Babylon, mother of all harlots. Now finish what you started."

MARS

when a baby was born in Rome / it was to the paterfamilias to decide / if he would raise
it up off the floor / where the midwife laid it / and give it his name forever / or have it
dropped by the trash heap / along the fetid river / for the rats, the dogs, the stars / or if the
baby was fortunate, anyone / chancing by in need of a slave /

would it surprise you to know / this latter happened more to infant boys / than girls, even,
of course, to the twins / those dreamers of the city of seven hills / but you know that story
already / the fig tree, the river bank, the moon /

how the wolf appeared and raised them up / in her jaws and carried them to dry / and
warm and dark, suckled them to sleep / and hushed their cries with her own / song of
forsakenness, and how some / years later, one would slay / his brother to sit on the chair of
glory / and give his name to all the paterfamilias of the realm /

of course, the word for she-wolf / and prostitute are the same in Latin / and lupanar is the
word for a cave / which is also a brothel, and any girl / without a husband in those days
/ would have needed fangs that could / snap bones in two, the ability / to vanish in a full
moon's light /

but since we're speaking here / of enclosure and asylum / of safeguarding from the
elements / and the appetites of blood-soaked men / let us remember the last garment /
Romulus ever wore, a swirling / cloak of thunder and hail and ash / a storm he could not
take off / a dress designed by the gods / to be his shield and refuge / out of which he never
could emerge / that boy, that lost one, that son

TIME OF THE ASSASSINS

Imagine that within this block of Thassian marble
        is the Ecstasy of St. Theresa
perfect, finished, but clotted
        by excess rock. Inside, the saint tears
and claws at that which is heaped up around her.
        If she cannot free the holy word
from her lips, the word and its power will die. Alas,
        you failed to imagine a chisel.

Of course the magic apple was not enough
        for the girl in the blue lingerie.
She left you a note, scrawled on the ash-smeared
        face of "Matinee D'Ivresse."
It reads, "My Love, I'm starved, you bastard
        Adios."
From now on you are an orphan sunspeck.
        A syllable on the lips of a hungry girl.
Now fill up the loveless world.

BOYHOOD IN ITHAKA

June in the hot garage
where the dank smoke whirled
where the raw meat dripped

where we the local prey
bumped *All Eyez On Me*
fresh out the packaging

where pop's car was ever
gone, where he left all his stupid
shit I don't know how to use

where our infant hearts were buried
in knee-high drums of lye, where
the blades in their mounted sheathes

sang louder than the trapped mosquitos
where we put on alien accents, rolled
our father's ghost in cigarillo shrouds

where your gun found its way
to my head, said 'cause the fuck
I say so.' Where the wettest

of the secrets stayed. That's
what I think of when I think of
home. Oil stain. Echo. A spent

round of sweat from your brow
exploding on the concrete floor
as if you were becoming

the mother of the war
when in fact you were
its most loved boy

II.

RESISTANCE

4 0 4   P A G E   N O T   F O U N D

Behind the internet we can see / is another internet, / the truer one. It eats / our wartime secrets, it records / the permutations of our slow-decaying / faces all day, each / and every night.

There was a writer who wrote / the Novel of Novels before / his hideous death. / That book was never found. / I will not tell you, "This book / is every book, recoded into one." / "To be known in perfect / understanding" is what it feels like / to read this book, so the story goes. / Some people, internet people, / believe the writer did not die, / he's secretly alive, still writing. / To raise himself again when we need him most. / Others have proof he was murdered / by the new government. / All of these people are important / fools. Zealots for the talmud of a dream.

Tonight I get offline / and walk the country, / looking in at every glowing face. / And who / these days, is anything but? / What with the air tasting like human chalk? / What with fear in every sinew of the radio wave. / Even the rats are hung up / on old ghost tales, / whispering in our walls about the great snake king / who sheds his mystic skin each night. / The instructions of their ancestors / coded upon his scales.

THE FATAL COMMISSION OF DESIRE

   I threw out the mouthwash and the white wine vinaigrette
caught myself redhanded in the pantry
banging failure in the dark. In the bath
   I did a charcoal, called it "Mortifications of Youth"
but its delusion came out blue.
The glans in my canvas spasm for the new.
Mardi Gras was yelling 'PINK ME!'
on the street below so I wrote
   TREMBLE A FALSE GOD on every mirror
got myself all dolled up in rags
and called a cab, threw my canvas
in a holster, fell downstairs into
   midnight rum, a delirium of giving in
and falling through.
I ended up dead at your
apartment
   in the museum. Every surface pristine
as past the rapture. Even the dust had risen.
Your fingers (the real thing) melting me
to the floor, which was waves
   which was India.
I took the pebble road across
the quiet continent of your voice.
You said, While you are not safe
 I am not safe... and so I slept
for thirty seconds, an era,

a whole moment where color was uproarious
again like in the '40s.
    I don't know anything but
    your hands are kind.
I owe you at least this sculpture
done in smoke—
you saved my only life.

WHEN THERE WERE BOTTLES
BY MY BED

At twelve I hid a cheap chianti
        in my brother's closet

cut school and spent the day
        observing myself slurp it from

the mirrors. I wore a monogrammed silk robe
        and a fedora (this is not made up)

on my back was a twelve hundred pound glass
        replica of Jesus Christ.

It was then that I carried Him
        (my lips) purple, the wine all gone

garage door rumbling up at five-fifteen
        to let my parent's car in

(the infernal wheel and thunder of)
        the gate of Hell. From then on

I belonged to no one, I could manifest
        at any of earth's coordinates

(in the guise of) anyone you've ever known, so long
        as the sloshing cup I held was never

the last. And how could I fail to turn
        the multiplying of my cups

into a ministry? A dithyramb to
        the dead god within me?

Once, a friend's mom came to our party
        and when we finished

(the good wine) she handed us her silver
        said go buy twelve more

and for a season we worshipped her
        in violence and song

and only later did we steal
        her car. The only thing

I ever feared was running out (that's why
        I kept it by my bed)

the way they sent the pharaohs to the realm
        of the dead with legs

of beef. (The human) sacrifices
        mattered, but they were not

the point, the point was to be
        eternally supple and full

swerving loose around the darkness
        once the door is (sealed).

THE BODY WILL SOON BE SUPERFLUOUS: A SYMPOSIUM

: The body remembers, yes, with much more clarity than the mind.

: So to speak.

: In a tuxedo, chasing a goose.

: The voice, an ejection from the body, negotiates that distance. Serves as courier between castles.

: It was New Years Eve, if I recall. A drunken retching body.

: One mourns its loss; one's feet curl beneath one's legs, which curl beneath one's hips. A concentrated, moral posture.

: I believe it's customary to blame Descartes.

: Are we not tired of pretending it is anything more than that most lethal of ferocities: hunger.

: The body of the ~~mother~~. The body of ~~Our Lord~~. The body ~~politic~~. The body ~~elec~~ you get it.

: The body of the goose was flayed, rinsed, chopped, its innards spooned out steaming into a pot, curried and boiled, the heart devoured raw.

: A mirror we fall into. A reflexive embodiment.

: A mode of universal bondage. Whether it
is Jeanne d'Arc or the boy outside the window in the womb.

: Yoke a star from its orbit. Make it walk the
dog.

: Of which burning is the most radical. The
most tragic. Thus most beautiful. To immo-
late.

: The constant being not flesh and bone but
breath, an unseen, all too often unacknow-
ledged unanimity.

: Only if the body's business is to satiate itself.

: Allow me to slip into something a bit more
fuckable. Allow me to poison myself to a dew-
y lush young and famous death.

: Neither necessary nor sufficient. The bod-
y born into a riot of sadness. Salted to taste.

THE DIRTY WAR

Savage thunder storms with possible rogue tornados. All Summer's Eve. We know too much science about this weather. I miss the 1970s the way you know that scary buffalo from your dream. Neither of us seen it in "real life." How you splashed out of bed into a crisis of loud river, the cold ghost of Sitting Bull paddling off in your canoe. Everyone fears the buffalo.

It's All Summer's Eve, the night sky licks its purple lips. We're down to our last can of cash. Rain chutes off the fire escape like villagers fleeing a warlord's raid. "O god, yes, fuck me," you say. Our ancestors avert their eyes. The neighbor man whose son was shot sobs harshly through the walls.

How I miss the sinew's sting on my fingers when I let go, the way the arrow cut through the sweet rafters of air to land dead center in the iris of my enemy. And you, trying to row your boat away from that goddamn buffalo, his big anger pummeling the water, snorting the water, him so real. Row little girl row.

PASSIM

He said he wore all black for the poor, the imprisoned, the conscripted, but come on now. When Johnny Cash got clean he wore a blue jean jacket, a crisp white shirt, sang Hallelujah. And behold. The poor still poor, the prisons swelled, and how many rich boys went to war—

As a young man, I changed clothes twice a day. Mornings I put on my rubber raincoat zipped above the mouth. When evening came I'd change into my beggar's raiment and return to the people I had seen that day to rob them a second time—

When Cash died we drank for three straight days. When we couldn't pay our tab, we zipped the barkeep in my raincoat, tied him to the juke. Somebody surrendered their last five bucks and played "Sunday Morning Coming Down" a dozen times as we left. I drank for another three days and seven years—

I got rich and then got poor. I robbed more men in prison than I ever did free. I was reborn eight times and killed myself eight more. I went and looked in every chest they pointed at but I never found the Lord our God. Hallelujah to the ruined and despised—

Tonight I sip black coffee and stitch a coat of different shades, watching rain drops slide down the glass like competing versions of time, one drop running past the others, back to the morning Cash died and I wept through the booze, because of the booze, because inside I felt nothing, the black fire of my heart ribboning on like the banner for a regiment of ghosts—

FINAL SOLILOQUY OF THE INTERIOR DECORATOR

Before she came over
   the very first time
he swept the hardwood floors
   and polished surfaces,
changed the sheets from gray
   to Persian red and flipped a corner back.

The living room table was cleared
   of take-out menus and functional pens,
precisely scattered with the *Paris Review*, *n+1*,
   a translation of Mann, with Habermas and Mayakovsky,
the *Well-Tempered Clavier* open to the D minor fugue,
   a new biography of Baldwin, a small blue candle.
Then, the dust was blown, swept with the heel
   of the hand.

The kitchen was scrubbed and sprayed;
   more candles, these in foot-tall glass
and bearing the prayer and image of La Virgen de Guadalupe
   were made to ring the table in a glowing horseshoe.
On the counter, a bowl of oranges, a book called
   Cooking in the Basque Country. He put Scriabin on the player
very low, opened the window so the gardenia
   scent crept in. It was after all the heart of summer.

There would be gardens hung from the rafters
   if only there were rafters.

He took down certain pictures, put up others,
    and finally hung the Miró print
in the hall above the spot where it had leaned
    against the wall for seven months. French-
pressed coffee. Expelled the garbage. Flicked
    the lightbulb in the lamp. Smoothed the corner
of the rug. Looked from end to end, was satisfied.
    She rang. He buzzed her up. In the mirror
by the door he saw his face begin to slide like the first
    chattering pebbles of the problem.

WAR AT HOME: BIRTHRIGHT

My dad's new gun was on the table
        in its tiny velcro holster

Wanna hold it? he said, the grip
        poking out like how

my older son sleeps now
        ankles bared and ready to alight

upon the action, his little heart racing
        as I sing to him.

I did not want to hold it I am not
        afraid of guns

I am afraid of the men
        in my family

holding guns I am afraid
        of anger that devours

whole suburban homes like the floods
        we get down here, like

the monsters of the deep in the bible,
        shadows that take boys

into their vast bellies while god
        the father looks

the other way and I'm afraid
    of the high fevers

my older son gets, the delirium
    he disappears into

how his eyes don't see me
    when he gets like that

his lips cracked, the red storms
    of virus in his cheeks

my sweet babe. For when me
    and your mama go walking

at night, explained my dad.
    But I had seen the man-size

whorl of shiny new paint
    in the hallway of his house

this last time I came home
    and I have seen the finger

of death touch fondly the trigger
    of our lives enough times

since I was big enough to sing
    which isn't so big

at all and I wonder
        what my dad saw

across the varnished wood from him
        and his new gun, meaning

there, in that house where the last
        thing anyone could ever bear

was to be seen I wonder if
        he hated me for grabbing

ahold of the table right then as if
        the floods were here again

as if the behemoth shadow moved across
        the windows just then

as if my only thought was how
        to save myself

III.

DÉTENTE

ALL ABOUT SHADOWS

Everything in its reverse—
        the April trees wake up with red and crumbling buds.
The field mouse chases the cat through the grass which bends
        the wind which shaves the mountain which smears
its pigment through the sky.
        Ash leaps into flame and the beaten, poorest
children dance at the feasts served in their honor.

        But this too falls apart.
The wine separates from the water which returns
        to the sea which returns to the dark.
Chorus voices fall to a shrill silence.
        Stones melt. A zero rises in the west, like when
you close your eyes and see a disc hovering
        in the orange corner of your mind. A glimmer
of sweetly unintelligible sound
        an oratorio far away and underground.
The river gathers up its long skirt.

        My shoes put me on and walk me down
to the hill where my father leans
        on a trenching spade.
But before he can dig,
        but before—

GHETTO NOCTURNE

late at night the storm begins to take
        the form of the capricious god
the one I read about and disbelieve in

I am skimming an important book
        so I can check it off the list
this is its own small kind of fear

down on the avenue below
        the bars are emptying out
the night's first fight begins

I hear a bottle smash, a man shriek
        "Do something then!" sirens come
go past, and I think, yes

we ought to, but I am not the kind
        who can, I have too much to
prepare for, too much in store, since

all my life I've been beside catastrophe
        the violence of men and weather
I've sought the heresy of higher ground

the night is a great breathing city
        and I am an animal taking breath
after harried breath, nothing more

you are somewhere out there
        Lord, not thinking about me
while I wait to be swept up

by the incommensurable tide
        while I wait for the body I can die in
to become this body

SAVAGE NAVIGATION

There are countries of the heart we find one by one

        and they are not of our choosing

We remember the cry of gulls and look up

        to see a hole in the brute sky

What used to keep us warm has trickled out

        Wind scours the plain

And there is too much snow for us to overtake

        our shadows quick as thieves

There is a thicket ahead that even light the color

        of tusk cannot escape

And spring is not more than winter

        And we have already been forgotten

So let our cries over the darkening plain fall long enough

        for the cold to dismantle the echo

Stand at the thicket's edge and call it the sea of reeds

        Then brother link your hand to mine

and we will feel our way like little beasts

        blind in the deadwood dark

ALMOST ANYWHERE IS NOT NEW YORK

He has seen red leaves that crumble from the trees
and turn the trickling curbside stream to ash
    and in most countries fall is the shower
    from which a gorgeous woman sings
while he, down the hall, sips tea.

Most of him does not happen right here or right now
    and this is a sad doctrine.

Almost no one is the minister of their own desire
    even and especially in fall
when still, in the intense mist
    of his own remembering heart
he plucks the tart high notes from the blackest branch.

MONK'S LOVE

would it be enough to have
new orleans rain
satur day

a red room, and Lady D to burn the spoon
of "Lover Man" till I'm as clean as she is
under one nude siren horn—

you in the nearby
cooking me some sugar
work all week in that mud

to get this dry
what do we know of speaking fire
and tasting honey?

there's a muted solo moon
inside my chest
lay your head right here

and listen to it rise.

WATERCLOCKS AND WHIRLING BUCKETS

What is the difference between thought

and feeling

when you're deep in the garden
reading in the summer afternoon

and a sound startles
you

say, a plastic bag
bothered by the whitefoot of a cat

so you look up, bidden
to the tree reciting itself in the west

oracular, a hundred feet tall
rusting yellow in the sun?

The leaves shatter hotly in the distance
a memory readies its chamber in the mind.

There is no such thing as time
yet time goes on.

You and what watches you
have seen all this before.

In the garden, everyone you have ever been
begins to rain.

WAR AT HOME: DIASPORA

I.

We were together
every morning of our lives
for the first long wash of years
until every day since then, when
  we were apart.

II.

They were together
in the story until
the firstborn slew the younger
due to an itch. Blood
on a rock. The sun,
the ground reddening.
            And then they were apart.

III.

We were together, brother,
in the bitter green mornings
stomachs ruined, knuckles raw
spun and trembling but even
twinned as bodies made of muscle
            and dread, death chasers, we were apart.

IV.

We were together
in the night of the gun
and the day of the fire
and the dawn when all the serpents
hatched in every nook of our dwelling
and since it was you who called
the serpents forth
I fled, and we
          were apart.

V.

In another story they
were together until
the hour came to be born
and then one of them knew one thing:
to war. Picture that tumult.
Upside down and strangling. Both
with such soft bodies, gelatinous
like minnows swirling in a glass,
the one grappling somehow into
the other. But the real reversals
began when both were out, in the light
      apart.

VI.

We were together
in the mind of God
when the idea of the
person was born. When
our mother closed her
eyes and prayed for one
blessing in two forms.
When they lowered our
mother into the greening
earth. None of that was enough
and we're apart.

VII.

Are we together here
in the bowl of this night?
Am I speaking to you or
once again about you?
Sometimes I think it's you
crying from the darkness of
that well. I can't get you out.
I can sit at the cusp and speak
of God all night. I can take off
        my coat and drop it in.

WESTPHALIA

You need to treat it
or it's gonna be all

weeds, says the older
mild-voiced dreadlocked

man who cuts my grass.
What if I light it all

on fire? I ask. Am I
allowed to do that?

He looks off for a long
while at the horizon

and finally says
Not yet.

PROGRESS REPORT

Another year and we have not cured climate, plague, or the police.

And we have not cured the problem of the salamanders.

And we have not cured the loneliness of paper grocery bags gone damp beneath the leaky sink
or the dread they give us when we see them there.

And we have not cured crow's feet, or actually we have, that one we cured, but we have not
cured altitude sickness or snow blindness or bad faith.

And we have not cured our oafishness or our vanity
we wear them both out to the herb garden to pick weeds.

The salamanders infiltrate the house via cracks in the molding. Once inside
they are prey to Sophie, the insane cat with half a tail.

We have not cured any type of blindness, come to think. All those painters
were they alive today, would be in the same predicament.

And we have not cured what waits for us in the tall, blonde, whispering grass.

At time of writing the stoplight at Bourbon and Desire awaits a cure.

The inexorable tantrums of space-time, the tendency of celestial bodies to drift and stretch
the rubber band of being, has not and will not be cured.

We have so far cured a lot of meat.

And the slaughtered salamanders gather dust, fossilize under the couch or behind the dresser until my
wife finds them. Her shriek disrupts the balance between sacred orders, us silent monks who live and
pray here: spider, dust-bunny, bacteria, the love poems of Ovid, myself.

And we have not cured once and for all the mildew in the shower.

There's no money in a cure for absent fathers, or drunk boorish fathers, or fathers who are scared
of their sons.

There is no cure for the stone in the Holy Father's kidney.

Nor have we cured tornadoes.

The salamander pops its red underneck out and in like a child pops her gum then scoots through a crevice between wood and brick. I cure the crevice with some caulk sealing too the salamander's destiny.

We have not cured the dirtiness of the damn dog.

My mother calls to say they've cured her foot. I say I thought it was your leg.

We have not cured the shepherd of his narcolepsy

nor the wolf his patience.

There is no cure for the drought—the fires come.

We have a cure for fire.

The cat leaps from the top of the armchair gallops through the hall around the corner over the linoleum parquet floor, ecstatic, wondrously adept and closing in.

There is no cure for what's about to happen.

IV.

REALIGNMENT

WHAT WE KNOW ABOUT BABIES

When the baby dreams of flying, the dog sleeping next to it also dreams of flying.

+

The baby's fussiness is not what it seems. He conducts a Byzantine choir in his mind. They are making numerous, unforgivable mistakes.

+

Babies are born knowing already the cardinal directions: to the north and west is Mother. To the east and south and to the Holy Land is Mother. To the prophet's cave, to the upper reach where the basalt flows and cools, to the dog star sliding in the liquid sky, and the beveled tip of every drop of rain, and even the warm root of the lote tree in Paradise, she is.

+

The original baby never ate, never slept, never cried or executed bodily functions of any kind. All subsequent babies persevere in the august shadow of this baby. That is why these activities are so fraught with effort, fear, and we must say it, rage. How sad this is, their merciless self-appraisal against an impossible standard.

+

All babies are born knowing some rudimentary Arabic, a little Greek. What they do not know is how when speaking one must slash one's meaning into pieces, an infinite rug divvied up for each solitary believer.

+

Some babies are assigned to cruel mothers, mothers who are mad, mothers who have drunk moonshine and left them out in the drowning rain. These babies do not pull rank or pass judgment, their wails are still experiments, a sounding-out to the unseen, unmanned borders of our city.

+

The more arduous the baby's journey into this realm of existence, the harder they must sleep, for it is only when asleep that they perform the necessary labor of forgetting the terrible faces of God.

+

Every baby who was ever born was born immortal. The dying is done by us.

REQUIEM

I understand why people / believe the dead are watching / over them. This is not what I believe / but I do understand. It's not an idea / but an intuition. / Not a looking down but a looking / with. You perceive their face / behind the sheer netting / of the world, fixed, / so whatever you see, they see / you seeing it. As long / as you pay attention // so do / they. They've become / so patient in death, / your perpetual witness. Mama / see my son? / His little feet a blur / over the grass

THEN FROM NOTHING, SOMETHING

My son is learning to feed himself. For breakfast we offer a variety of foods but he will only
accept beans. He smears the beans on his face, in his hair, sails the bowl over my head into the
wall. It's how they learn.

> Like any writer, the Angel of History
> prays her work is beautiful
> will ultimately resolve
> in a beautiful form
> Were this even possible
> it would be unforgivably naive

I am alerted to the worst humanitarian crisis since WWII by a podcast this a.m. Famine in
South Sudan, Nigeria, Somalia, Yemen. Twenty million near starvation, mostly children and
their mothers. Some eat wild roots, others the leaves of water lilies. Their men already killed
in the fighting. After war, the wells run dry, cholera swims in the putrid dregs, a man fills his
pail for the family who cannot last another day without a sip. Then sits by as the baby dies, his
only daughter curls up with the baby and after a night of no tears dies. His wife dies, sister dies,
second youngest boy. After everyone in his village is dead, he gets up and begins to walk. I read
about this crisis on my phone at a gas station. Make a 'donate' button on my Facebook page.

> The Angel of History does not
> think dialectically
> she does not think as an ironist thinks
> she does not think at all
> The Angel of History writes

She writes with her bruised hands, her feet
red from the silt
of the river where she stands and drags
through the mud
a crooked bone

Once, when my boy was six months old, he became very sick all of a sudden and I held him to my breast and felt the chaos close my throat, felt rubble in my lungs. His eyes were open when he went limp, but he did not see me. Then I died. I was standing, holding his body which weighed nothing, as if there was nothing inside him, I yelled his name many times, I yelled it twenty million times, but I had died. He couldn't see that I was dead—he couldn't see at all. I dialed 9-1-1. In minutes, eleven city firemen, their ladder truck, and an ambulance arrived. They had my boy. They stepped around my body. Some of them were still trainees. When their captain bounced my son on his lap and said, "What beautiful blue eyes" I fell to my knees and was resurrected.

Sometimes the Angel of History worries
that what she writes is too incredible
Such as the passage about a man
who flees Hiroshima on foot and makes it
just in time to Nagasaki

I go and pick up the donuts. When I get home my little boy shrieks with joy, kicks his dirty little toes. Pasta spills from his hair. His mother says, "Try some peas."

The Angel of History writes about hunger
                    Ten million women on their knees for bread
Their voices like sirens like ships crashing like the sea in flames
                    God is merciful
          God is good.

          Because of her position
in the celestial bureaucracy
    the Angel of History never had children
              She doesn't understand what it feels like
to offer a spoonful of broth
    to a child who is too hungry
                    to swallow
          Or what it's like to know
                              after that child is dead
after you've held him in your arms and felt
          the nothing of his weight
                    that you are still alive
that broth is nothing in this world
          It's merely where you begin
                        what you leave in the bowl
              after you're full

ELEGY FOR MY FRIEND WHO IS IN GOOD HEALTH, THE POET EDWARD T.

Or Eduardo, as Mary K called you
I'm sitting here thinking how we'll all
be dead one day. You, me, and Mary K.

My dog has the cone around her neck.
I just had her spayed and we're sitting
here quiet like that April afternoon

you showed up at my door an angel of
grief and could barely say it. "Dilly died."
I'm sitting here laughing at the first time

I saw you in the snow with that sweet, enormous
leopard hound haunting Westcott St., two wary
souls like some digression out of Gogol.

Dilly, named for Daedalus, last link to the life
you had with your ex-wife. You carried her leash
with you, loose: one final walk. I mean

fuck. I don't know how you did that.
My pup rests her cone on my lap and cries.
She only knows the right-now of despair.

One thing we always were, Ed, was un-
despairing men. I'm sitting here thankful for
the barstool I fell off of after shattering

the pint glass on the floor to make a point
about rhetoric, and how you picked me up
off my back and told me to open my fool eyes.

"Dilly died," as you fell inside my house,
pushed past me to the whiskey's mouth
and turned the bagpipe dirge to a devils' roar.

And we ate that fucking whiskey, every drop
out in the mud of my front yard, staggering
wild, crying arduously to the Irish whistles

and I was afraid of you. Because after all
Ed, you're the one who puked, right there
on the front steps. And I'm the one who

needed to get sober. The whole wake long
your eyes were wet and blue like Dilly's
eyes, wet with the fidelity of mud. No love

had ever washed me out as pure as you were
then. Ed, if we persist we'll find a better way
to say all this. Probably we'll need each other,

a call and response, a catechism written in water.
I'm thinking of the dream I once had where you
called to me from a hospital bed, the cancer paling

your lips and wasting your greyhound
body into inert mounds of bed linen.
How I sat down beside you and wept

for once, in the cold of your plain sight.
But shit. You're the one who quit smoking.
I am trying to say thanks, Ed, for being

the one who let me see that this sweet dog
on my lap will die one day, and my wife
who sings nearby will die one day

and I will die too, and in that knowledge
lies the first principle of reckless love,
the seat of all virtue, and more.

I just got off the phone with Mary
and when she said, "How goes it with
Eduardo?" I told her you are skeptical

and true as dirt, that you're a poet who
prefers to write in graveyards, which
means you'll live for god damn ever.

AFTER A YEAR SOBER

Because it is raining
all the dogs are sad.
The cats have found themselves a spot to sleep.
In my city winter slips its ring over the last unwilling root.
In Paris, César Vallejo dies again
and again I have decided not
to drink for one more day
which means the bare trees out the window
weep for their own mysterious purposes
the tongue of the candle utters its new sura.
I am alone. Not the way I was in the tavern
but the way I was at birth—
blinded by a luminescent haze
lifted to its source
and listening to a voice that is the first voice
sing.

BOOK OF MOUNTAINS, WOODS, SPRINGS, LAKES, RIVERS, BOGS OR MARSHES, AND NAMES OF THE SEA

for Julian

All the plants I've ever owned have prematurely died.
Began to droop, in fact, the day I brought them home.
Organic life has never flourished in my care. What has?
Coffee, books, soul music, prints of Picassos, clothes
made of wool, little ivory statues of the buddha, lamps,
tamales, maps, the voices of friends arguing over politics,
over literature, over cities, over love. I will note the dog
seems fine. But historically I am no good or wise custodian
of things that breathe. And so, when your mother returned
to work, leaving you in my care from nine to five, each hour
was a gauntlet of probable calamity, of shameful fear that you
would break your skull, vomit, choke, stop breathing, turn
a sudden red or blue, and I would not know why. That all
I've neglected to learn about life would cost us yours.

       But my son, today, when you wobbled to your feet
and roared, wild eyed, like a little god calling the green world
up from the murk, I gathered our brand new tools: water, sun,
sweet air for the limbs to clutch, and if and when these fail,
the words you'll need to forgive me with.

WAR AT HOME: HAVEN

for Case

I do regret that we never smoked
crack. In fact it puzzles me, like how
we never learned to skate. Why not?
We loved, above all else, to be above
all else, carving up the milky way
surging bug-eyed on a single vector,
two shots from one astronomical
gun. "How're you two little angels?"
your mother always said, even when
her whole head was in flames, her
voice an undulating jungle, according
to the drugs I was on, even when
the only thing that could be said
for us was, "We are not on crack
yet," though you were a few times
nearly dead from powder, me, later,
and more than a few from booze.

I'm surprised that anyone outlived
her, even us, her boys, who she brought
waffles to in bed and cleaned up after
well into our teens, when what we slept
off wasn't basketball and laser tag
but scorched brain tissue and bloody
mouthwalls, apocalyptic visions
on the waters, like that night she caught

us on the beach house roof at four a.m.
trying to milk the stars and detonate
the sea with our eggs. "Look at the great
heaving fertility," we called to her, pupils
like black suns, "Can you see the explosions
we have sown in the body of God?"
"Come down from there," she said, "you
little fucking hellions," but without real
rancor, for whatever we did, she was pleased
we did it together. "I can't get you idiots
out of jail in Mexico," she liked to say
but of course she easily could have,
or anything else that needed doing, but for
keeping herself alive into old age. I never
saw her hair gray. She never saw my
second son.

Why, brother, is she gone? Once
for Mother's Day, I got her a book
called *Raising Your Spirited Child*.
You were already in AA. I'd never
seen her laugh so hard. What if
we'd have known a little sooner
that she was sick? A mercy
of months, or even weeks. I know
you wouldn't wish for that, to know
your mother was dying any longer

than you had to, which was ten days.
But I wanted to sit with her while
her eyes were still open. I wanted
to read her a poem. I wanted her to say
"Isn't that marvelous?" one more time.
I'm sitting today on the shore of a lake
in upstate New York and gulls
are crying overhead and what I want
to remember is how the tropic sun felt
on my feet on the deck of her house
on Galveston Bay when we were twelve
but I can't. So much has been burned
out of my mind. Give me some
of your memory, please. A moment real
as a ripe berry burst on the tongue.
Is such a feat still possible? Once,
it was. We used to move as one body
skimming barefoot over the baking flats
of that island, palm trees bowing
in the bay winds, glitter on the water,
her voice calling us in.

TOWARD A KINGDOM OF ENDS

When I see them as an end-in-themselves
  I have seven mothers
and the languages they speak
   are untranslatable and liquid
as the rings of a planet burning seven ways
  to the same point.

When I see him as an end-in-himself
   the man on the corner
is my father, and the dollar he takes
    was his already, his fingers tucked it beneath
the pillow of my crib one night to satisfy
  the gods who made me wail.

When I see it as an end-in-itself
   the bluebird that dies,
dies.
   The boy who searches for it in the blue leaves
singing softly
  is a wound in the magnificent flesh of time.
I would pay any god to let me
   take his place.

ACKNOWLEDGEMENTS

For a debut as long in the works as this one, it would be safer to write an autobiography than to try and acknowledge everyone to whom I'm grateful. But here goes.

To my mother Gloria Brunt, who knew that books would be my salvation, and so surrounded me with them from the first day. And to the mother who was not mine and mothered me anyway, Lecia Karr Scaglione, how I miss you, first reader and last word—if I have a voice, it's a gift from you both.

To Case Scaglione, my brother in art and life, this book expresses what we lived through side by side. To Mary Karr who opens the doors, and if they still won't open, demonstrates how to walk through walls. To Phil Lamarche, who showed me twelve ways to stay alive and how to honor all that we've been given.

To Brooks Haxton, who sat me in his kitchen and patiently aimed his genius at poems much poorer than these so that these could eventually emerge. To my workshop at the Syracuse MFA, Carroll Beauvais, RS Mengert, Jasmine Santana, Daniel Moriarty (RIP), and my comrade Edward Tato—the folks who first showed me what poems and poets really do, and why. To all my beloved former teachers and current colleagues at SU—Arthur Flowers, George Saunders, Dana Spiotta, John Dee, Mona Awad, Bruce Smith, Chris Kennedy, Michael Burkard, and Sarah Harwell. To my mentors at the University of Houston who read and encouraged my earliest attempts, and who later became friends and colleagues, especially John Harvey, Gabriela Maya, Bill Monroe, and Leslie Marenchin (RIP).

To Hayan Charara and Brandon Lamson, longtime champions and resurrectors of so many versions of these poems and life cycles of this book—it simply wouldn't exist without you both. To Mikael Awake and Martin De Leon, my ride-or-die writer brethren till kingdom come. To Andrew Milward, Monika Gehlawat, Ellis Purdie, Kent Quaney, Eddie Malone, Joe Holt, Jennifer Brewington, Laura Bandy, and everyone from the University of Southern Mississippi Center for Writers for the literary support and friendship they gave me in my newly recovering but still over-the-top latter youth.

To the friends who have aided and inspired and held my hand along the path, Kaveh Akbar, Leslie Jamison, Erin Williams, Joy Priest, Afaa Weaver, Elizabeth Crane, Melissa Febos, Chase Berggrun, Alex Watson, K. Iver, Bernadette Murphy, Benjamin Price, John Freyer, Ganavya Doraiswamy, Kasey Anderson, Himanshu Suri, Krissy Shields, Erin Noehre, Solmaz Sharif, Carl Erik Fisher, and Dev Milburn.

To my parents, and to Michael Frontain, Daniel Magariel, Christopher Cook, Elaine Frontain Bryant, Brian Braskich, Ricardo Nuila, Tyler Dorholt, Wendy Paris, Georgia Popoff, Vishal Agraharkar, Sharlie Velasco, Chris Glasgow, Ray Hafner, John Curry, Linda Coney, Dalton & Carol Sue Krueger, and all who have fed me, read me, loved me, and loaned me their truck over these years.

To Timothy Liu, Sarah Wetzel, and the team at Saturnalia Books for being the people who saw a real live book in these pages and lent their labor, time, and brilliance to make it so.

To the Rooms and everyone I've ever met there for saving my only life years ago, and today.

Finally to Chanelle Benz, who is that life, and its splendor. To Julian, the wonder who makes it grow beyond my wildest imaginings. And to Nico, who is the light.

I would like to thank the editors of the publications in which these poems first appeared, sometimes in earlier versions and with different titles. "War At Home: Haven" in *The Nation*, "What We Know About Babies" in *Fugue*, "Kingdom of Ends" in *The Cincinnati Review* and on the Academy of American Poets website poets.org, "404 Page Not Found" in *Copper Nickel*, "The Metaphysician Calls His Mother From Jail" and "Water Clocks and Whirling Buckets" in *Meridian*,

"All About Shadows" in *Drunken Boat*, "Scherzo for Children" in *Bat City Review*, "Final Soliloquy of the Interior Decorator" in *Ovenbird*, "The Commission of Desire" in *Tirage Monthly*, "Passim" in *Product*, "See See Rider," "Dark Was the Night Cold Was the Ground," "Boom Boom Out Go the Lights" and "Honey Hush" in *Sol Literary Magazine*.

ABOUT THE AUTHOR

Christopher Brunt's poetry, fiction, and essays have been featured in *Ploughshares*, *The Nation*, *Oxford American*, *Fugue*, *Meridian*, *Copper Nickel*, the *Cincinnati Review*, and other magazines. He has been a finalist for the Alma Book Award, the Marsh Hawk Poetry Prize, and the St. Lawrence Book Award, and shortlisted for the Christopher Smart Poetry Prize. Born and raised in Houston, Texas, he has an MFA from Syracuse University and a PhD in English from the University of Southern Mississippi. He currently teaches literature and creative writing at Syracuse University, and is the creator and host of *PODRE*, a podcast on fatherhood, recovery, and the creative life.

War at Home was printed in Adobe Garamond

www.saturnaliabooks.org

Printed in the USA
CPSIA information can be obtained
at www.ICGtesting.com
CBHW020559301024
16628CB00026B/563